SCIENCE EXPLORER

JUNIOR

Think Like a Scientist in the Gym

by Christine Taylor-Butler

CHERRY LAKE PUBLISHING · ANN ARBOR, MICHIGAN

Published in the United States of America by Cherry Lake Publishing
Ann Arbor, Michigan
www.cherrylakepublishing.com

Content Editor: Robert Wolffe, EdD, Professor of Teacher Education,
Bradley University, Peoria, Illinois

Design and Illustration: The Design Lab

Photo Credits: Page 5, ©MaszaS/Shutterstock, Inc.; page 8, ©Dmitriy
Shironosov/Shutterstock, Inc.; page 12, ©Elena Korn/Shutterstock,
Inc.; page 16, ©Mark Herreid/Dreamstime.com; page 17, ©cabania/
Shutterstock, Inc.; page 19, ©Stephen Mcsweeny/Shutterstock, Inc.;
page 21, ©Suzanne Tucker/Dreamstime.com; page 22, ©Panos
Karapanagiotis/Shutterstock, Inc.; page 23, ©Georgios Kollidas/
Dreamstime.com; page 26, ©Anthony Baggett/Dreamstime.com; page
29, ©JJ pixs/Shutterstock, Inc.

Library of Congress Cataloging-in-Publication Data
Taylor-Butler, Christine.
  Think like a scientist in the gym/by Christine Taylor-Butler.
     p. cm.—(Science explorer junior)
  Includes bibliographical references and index.
  ISBN 978-1-61080-163-8 (lib. bdg.)
  1. Physics—Experiments—Juvenile literature. 2. Schools—Exercises
and recreations—Juvenile literature. I. Title. II. Series.
  QC25.T39 2011
  507.8—dc22   2010053575

Cherry Lake Publishing would like to acknowledge the work
of The Partnership for 21st Century Skills. Please visit
www.21stcenturyskills.org for more information.

Printed in the United States of America
Corporate Graphics Inc.
July 2011
CLFA09

TABLE OF CONTENTS

How Does That Work?

Science experiments can help you learn how your body moves.

Have you ever looked at something and wondered, "How does that work?" Scientists do that all the time. Even in a school gymnasium.

You can use physics knowledge to get better at sports.

A gym is a great place for sports. You can also use a gym to learn a lot about science. How fast can you run? How far can you throw? How high can you jump? Scientists study **physics** to find the answers to these questions. Athletes can use this information to improve their skills.

STEP-BY-STEP

You can get your own answers by thinking like a scientist. Go step by step. You may have to repeat some steps as you go.

1. Observe what is going on.
2. Ask a question.
3. Guess the answer. This is called a **hypothesis**.
4. Design an **experiment** to test your idea.
5. Gather materials to test your idea.
6. Write down what happens.
7. Make a **conclusion**.

Don't forget your notepad.

Use words and numbers to write down what you've learned. It's okay if the experiment doesn't work. Try changing something, and then do the experiment again.

Write down everything you notice.

GET THE FACTS

Libraries have information on any subject you can think of.

Scientists look for facts before they start an experiment. They use this information as a place to start.

Where can you find information? A library is filled with books, magazines, and science videos that can help you. You can talk to a coach or an athlete. You can visit a museum, too.

You can also find facts on the Internet. Be careful. Not everything on the Internet is the truth. Ask an adult to help you find the best places to look for information.

Coaches can help you with anything you need in the gym.

Breathe Deep

Playing sports is hard work.

ASK A QUESTION

When you play sports, your heart beats faster. Your breathing gets faster, too.

What happens to your body when you take a break?

When you get tired, you stop to catch your breath. When you sit down, your heart slows down. What is happening?

A scientist named Leonardo da Vinci had a big idea. He knew that when people worked hard, they breathed faster. He guessed that breathing fast helped pump more blood to your muscles. His idea was wrong, but he was close.

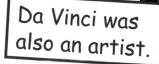
Da Vinci was also an artist.

Feel for a pulse in your wrist.

When you exercise, you breathe hard to give your blood more **oxygen**. Your heart beats faster to pump the blood to your body. A **pulse** is a way to measure your heart rate. What are some good places on your body to measure your pulse? Try your neck, wrist, and ankle. Which one works best?

DO AN EXPERIMENT

You will need a stopwatch, a pencil, and a notepad.

Measure your pulse before you play a sport. Use a clock or stopwatch. Count the number of beats in 60 seconds. Write down the number. Measure your pulse after 5 minutes of exercise. Measure it again after 10 minutes of exercise. Is there a difference?

Measure your pulse when you're finished playing. Measure it again after 10 minutes of resting. Did it return to normal? Scientists like to repeat their experiments to see if they get the same answer. What happens if you try your experiment again? What is your conclusion?

Before exercise: 88
5 minutes of exercising: 132
10 minutes of exercising: 153
After exercise: 120
10 minutes after exercise: 92

Keep detailed notes as you experiment.

Track It!

Close races are very exciting.

ASK A QUESTION

Have you ever watched a track meet at school? Runners win a medal by going faster than anyone else in the race. Some runners work hard to be faster than anyone else in the world.

Do girls run faster than boys? Do short runners run as fast as tall ones? Can you run faster in your bare feet or with shoes? How would you test your ideas? Where can you find clues to help you get started?

Do you think all girls are fast runners?

Scientists measure how far an object travels. They also measure how much time the trip takes. They use math to find out how fast the object moves for each unit of time. This is called **speed**.

Math can help you figure out how fast you are.

speed = distance ÷ time

So if you ran 12 feet in 6 seconds, your speed would be 2 feet per second.

12 feet ÷ 6 seconds = 2 feet per second

Runners work hard to keep getting better.

Athletes use this information to improve their speed. They run over and over again to find their fastest time. They change materials in their experiment. Sometimes they change shoes. Sometimes they wear lighter clothes.

Make sure you have everything you'll need.

Gather a stopwatch, a calculator, a pencil, a notepad, a tape measure, and a few friends. Measure a long line on the gym floor. Write down the number of feet. Ask a friend to run from one end of the line to the other. How many seconds did it take? Calculate your friend's speed in feet per second. Can your friend run faster next time? What is that person's best speed?

Now ask all of the friends to race each other. Who is fastest? Who is slowest? Try the experiment again without shoes. Does that change your results? Would the results change if you raced on the sidewalk? How about in the grass? What did you learn?

How do track shoes affect a runner's speed?

Drop It!

Aristotle made many important discoveries.

ASK A QUESTION

A long time ago, a scientist named Aristotle had a big idea. He guessed that heavy objects drop faster than light ones. Do you think he was correct?

A scientist named Galileo Galilei had a different idea. He guessed that all objects fall at the same speed. It didn't matter how much they weighed. He dropped objects from a tower in Italy. Do you think Galileo was correct?

Did Galileo have the right idea about gravity?

DO AN EXPERIMENT

Find a basketball, a soccer ball, and a tennis ball. Ask permission to drop them from a tall height. Ask two friends for help. Drop each ball at the same time. Which ball hits the floor first? Try again. Which scientist was correct, Aristotle or Galileo?

Make sure you drop the balls at the same time.

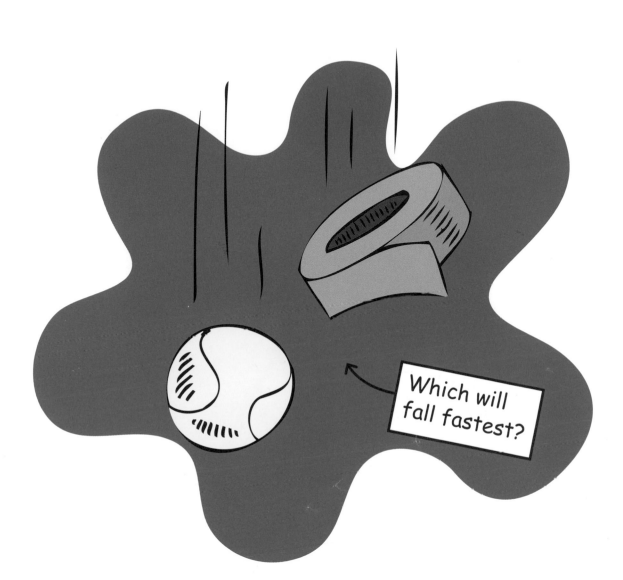

Does the experiment work if you throw one ball at an angle and drop the other straight down? What happens if you repeat the experiment with a ball and a roll of tape? Does it work with any object? What is your conclusion?

Your Big Idea!

Newton's discoveries helped explain how gravity works.

A scientist named Isaac Newton saw an apple fall from a tree. He wondered if an invisible **force** pulled the apple to the ground. This force is called **gravity**.

Gravity works like a magnet. Gravity helps you stay on the ground when you walk. It pulls you toward the center of Earth. Without gravity, you might float off into space.

Gravity makes all objects fall 32 feet (9.8 meters) in the first second. It turns out Galileo was right!

Be thankful that gravity keeps your feet on the ground!

DO AN EXPERIMENT

You can measure how fast something falls to the ground.

Gather a tape measure, a notepad, a pencil, a stopwatch, and a ball. You can use any kind of ball for this experiment.

Ask an adult to climb up high enough so that the ball can be dropped 7 feet (2 m). Use your stopwatch to measure how long it takes the ball to

What kind of experiment will you do next?

fall to the ground. Use a calculator to divide 7 feet (2 m) by the number of seconds. What is the speed?

Now it's time for you to think like a scientist. Ask an adult to help you drop the ball from an even higher place. Now try the experiment with a lighter or heavier ball. What happens to your measurements?

Do you think the experiment would work the same in space? Where could you go to get information? What will your next big idea be?

GLOSSARY

conclusion (kuhn-KLOO-zhuhn) the answer or result of an experiment

experiment (ik-SPER-uh-ment) a test of your idea

force (FORS) a type of energy that makes something move

gravity (GRAV-i-tee) the force that pulls things toward the center of Earth and keeps them from floating away

hypothesis (hye-PAH-thi-sis) a guess

oxygen (AHK-si-juhn) a gas with no smell or color

physics (FIZ-iks) the science of matter and energy

pulse (PUHLS) a measurement of how fast a heart is beating

speed (SPEED) a measure of the rate at which something is moving

FOR MORE INFORMATION

BOOKS

Ballard, Carol. *What Is My Pulse? Blood and Circulation*. Chicago: Heinemann Raintree, 2011.

Hollihan, Kerrie Logan. *Isaac Newton and Physics for Kids: His Life and Ideas with 21 Activities*. Chicago: Chicago Review Press, 2009.

Mitton, Jacqueline. *Galileo*. New York: Oxford University Press, 2009.

WEB SITES

NOVA—Galileo's Experiments
www.pbs.org/wgbh/nova/pisa/expe_flash_1.html
Try the activities on this site to learn more about Galileo's experiments.

Science Kids: Why Don't People on the "Other Side" of the Earth Fall Off?
www.cs.dartmouth.edu/farid/sciencekids/gravity.html
Visit this site to learn more about gravity.

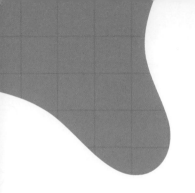

INDEX

ABOUT THE AUTHOR

Christine Taylor-Butler is the author of more than 60 books for children. A graduate of MIT she enjoys conducting science experiments and finding the connection to real life applications. She currently lives in Kansas City, Missouri.